First World War
and Army of Occupation
War Diary
France, Belgium and Germany

58 DIVISION
Divisional Troops
Royal Army Medical Corps
2/1 Home Counties Field Ambulance
1 September 1915 - 29 February 1916

WO95/2997/1

The Naval & Military Press Ltd
www.nmarchive.com
Published in association with The National Archives

Published by

The Naval & Military Press Ltd

Unit 10 Ridgewood Industrial Park,

Uckfield, East Sussex,

TN22 5QE England

Tel: +44 (0) 1825 749494

www.naval-military-press.com

www.nmarchive.com

This diary has been reprinted in facsimile from the original. Any imperfections are inevitably reproduced and the quality may fall short of modern type and cartographic standards.

© **Crown Copyright**
Images reproduced by permission of The National Archives, London, England, 2015.

Contents

Document type	Place/Title	Date From	Date To
Heading	WO95/2997-1		
Heading	U K 58 Division (HC) F From 67 (HC) Division 2/1 Home Counties Fld Amb 1915 Sep-1916 Feb		
Heading	War Diary of Major A.T. Falwasser Commanding 2/1st Home Counties Fd Ambce R.A.M.C.T. From September 1st 1915 To September 30th 1915		
War Diary	Tunbridge Wells	01/09/1915	30/09/1915
Heading	War Diary Of Major A.T. Falwasser Commanding 2/1st Home Counties Fd Ambce R.A.M.C.T. From October 1.15 To October 31.15 (Volume 1.)		
War Diary	Tunbridge Wells	01/10/1915	18/10/1915
War Diary	East Grinstead	19/10/1915	19/10/1915
War Diary	Redhill	20/10/1915	31/10/1915
Heading	War Diary Of Lt. Colonel A.T. Falwasser Commanding 2/1st Home Counties Field Ambulance R.A.M.C. T. From November 1st. 1915. To November 30th 1915.		
War Diary	Redhill	03/12/1915	03/12/1915
Heading	War Diary Of Lieut Colonel A.T. Falwasser Commanding 2/1st Home Counties Field Ambulance R.A.M.C. T.F. From Dec 1st. 1915 To Dec 31st. 1915. (Volume 1.)		
War Diary	Redhill	31/12/1915	31/12/1915
Heading	War Diary Of Lieut Colonel A.T. Falwasser Commanding 2/1st Home Counties Field Ambce R.A.M.C. T.F. From Jan 1st 1916 To Jan 31st 1916 (Volume 2)		
War Diary	Redhill	11/01/1916	22/02/1916
War Diary	Earlswood	22/02/1916	22/02/1916
War Diary	Ipswich	22/02/1916	29/02/1916

WO 95/29971

UK
58 DIVISION (HC)
from 67 (HC) DIVISION

2/1 HOME COUNTIES FLD AMB

1915 SEP — 1916 FEB

CONFIDENTIAL

War Diary
of
Major A.T. FALWASSER
Commanding 2/1st Home Counties Fd Ambce
R.A.M.C. T.

from September 1st 1915 to September 30th 1915

WAR DIARY
or
INTELLIGENCE SUMMARY

(Erase heading not required.)

Army Form C. 2118.

Instructions regarding War Diaries and Intelligence Summaries are contained in F.S. Regs., Part II. and the Staff Manual respectively. Title pages will be prepared in manuscript.

Hour, Date, Place	Summary of Events and Information	Remarks and references to Appendices
9 AM 1.9.15 TUNBRIDGE WELLS	Field work at BROADWATER FOREST	
2 PM "	Lectures on Med Army Equipt, in Medical arrangemts in the field & on Nursing Orderlies	ADS
9 AM 2.9.15 TUNBRIDGE WELLS	Route march with wagons loaded according to tables to MAYFIELD. Dinner cooked in field. Field work carried out.	ADS
9 AM 3.9.15 TUNBRIDGE WELLS	Field work at BROADWATER FOREST. Lectures on Sanitation + on organisation of a Field Ambce.	ADS
9 AM 4.9.15 TUNBRIDGE WELLS	Bathing Parade for all ranks. Lecture on First Aid	ADS
13 AM 5.9.15 TUNBRIDGE WELLS	Sunday service in CAMMON with 100 & Sutty Rifles 200 & Rifle Bde + 17 (UPS) Ser Lspool R	ADS

Army Form C. 2118.

WAR DIARY
or
INTELLIGENCE SUMMARY.
(Erase heading not required.)

Instructions regarding War Diaries and Intelligence Summaries are contained in F.S. Regs., Part II. and the Staff Manual respectively. Title pages will be prepared in manuscript.

Hour, Date, Place	Summary of Events and Information	Remarks and references to Appendices
9 AM 6.9.15 TUNBRIDGE WELLS	Lecture by Major Lidell on Grenades, 3 lectures on Front Aid.	
2 PM	Route March LANGTON – SPELDHURST – PENSHURST – SOUTH BOROUGH. A.J.S	
7 AM 7.9.15 TUNBRIDGE WELLS	Field work at RUSHALL COMMON.	
1 PM	Lecture on Saluting.	
2 PM	Night work PEMBURY – KIPPINGS CROSS – FRANT A.J.S	
7 AM 8.9.15 TUNBRIDGE WELLS	Field Pulley Exercises. Physical Drill & First Aid Lecture at 11.30 a.m.	
1 PM	Lecture on Holland, organization & on Illustration of War. A.J.S	
9 AM 9.9.15 TUNBRIDGE WELLS	Field work at BROADWATER FOREST. A.J.S	

(73989) W.4141—463. 400,000. 9/14. H.&J.,Ltd. Forms/C. 2118/10.

Army Form C. 2118.

WAR DIARY
or
INTELLIGENCE SUMMARY.
(Erase heading not required.)

Instructions regarding War Diaries and Intelligence Summaries are contained in F.S. Regs., Part II. and the Staff Manual respectively. Title pages will be prepared in manuscript.

Hour, Date, Place	Summary of Events and Information	Remarks and references to Appendices
9 AM 10.9.15 TUNBRIDGE WELLS	Short march to RUSHALL COMMON.	
2 PM "	Packing wagons & leather n Sanitation	ADS
9 AM 11.9.15 TUNBRIDGE WELLS	Bathing Parade lecture on Trench Act.	
9.30 AM 12.9.15 TUNBRIDGE WELLS	Divine Service on COMMON with 100th Infantry Bde. & attached Units	ADS
9 AM 13.9.15 TUNBRIDGE WELLS	Stretcher & bearer drill on COMMON.	
2 PM "	Route March LANGTON – PENSHURST – MODHURST – SOUTHBOROUGH	ADS
9 AM 14.9.15 TUNBRIDGE WELLS	Lectures on Field First Aid, Splints & bandaging wagons.	
2 PM "	Stretcher drill on COMMON.	
2 PM "	Night march HAWKENBURY – PEMBURY – KIPPINGS CROSS – FRANT STATION.	ADS

WAR DIARY
or
INTELLIGENCE SUMMARY.

Army Form C. 2118.

(Erase heading not required.)

Instructions regarding War Diaries and Intelligence Summaries are contained in F. S. Regs., Part II and the Staff Manual respectively. Title pages will be prepared in manuscript.

Hour, Date, Place	Summary of Events and Information	Remarks and references to Appendices
9 AM 15.9.15 TUNBRIDGE WELLS	Office work at RUSTHALL COMMON.	
2 PM	Orders on Sanitation & Notifying Epidemic.	
9 AM 16.9.15 TUNBRIDGE WELLS	9.00 work at BROADWATER FOREST & drawing station A) 5 Hospital. A conference held. Orders carried in detail. A) 5 Inspection of Eastern Hospitals by Surgeon General COLLING RAMC Central Force A) 5	
9 AM 17.9.15 TUNBRIDGE WELLS	Office work on COMMON. A) 5	
2 PM	Lectures on Sanitation & on Medical Organization in the field. A) 5	
9 AM 18.9.15 TUNBRIDGE WELLS	Riding Practice. Letters opened & dealt with. A) 5	
9.30 AM 19.9.15 TUNBRIDGE WELLS	Route march on COMMON with 2nd/4th London Field Ambce. Inspected 1st/4th RE N 2 (1st & 2nd) A) 5 Co. A) 5	

WAR DIARY
or
INTELLIGENCE SUMMARY.
(Erase heading not required.)

Army Form C. 2118.

Instructions regarding War Diaries and Intelligence Summaries are contained in F.S. Regs., Part II. and the Staff Manual respectively. Title pages will be prepared in manuscript.

Hour, Date, Place	Summary of Events and Information	Remarks and references to Appendices
9 AM 20.9.15 TUNBRIDGE WELLS	Field work & longer drill on COMMON. Seven light draught horses read from Remount Dépôt Reserve.	
1 PM	Route March FRANT STATION — BAYHAM — WADHURST — FRANT.	ADS
9 AM 21.9.15 TUNBRIDGE WELLS	Stretcher & longer drill on COMMON.	
	Lectures on Sanitation & HH Q.O.	
2 PM		
7 PM	Night march & field work at BROADWATER FOREST	ADS
9 AM 22.9.15 TUNBRIDGE WELLS	Field work at RUSHALL.	
2 PM	Lecture Medical & Surgical Equipment. Packing wagons.	
9 AM 23.9.15 TUNBRIDGE WELLS	Route March & Field work at BROADWATER FOREST. Divine service held in field.	ADS
9 AM 24.9.15 TUNBRIDGE WELLS	Field work on COMMON. Lectures on Sanitation & on Medical organization.	ADS

Army Form C. 2118.

WAR DIARY
or
INTELLIGENCE SUMMARY.
(Erase heading not required.)

Instructions regarding War Diaries and Intelligence Summaries are contained in F.S. Regs., Part II. and the Staff Manual respectively. Title pages will be prepared in manuscript.

Hour, Date, Place	Summary of Events and Information	Remarks and references to Appendices
9 AM. 25.9.15 TUNBRIDGE WELLS	Battting Parade Lecture & practical First-Aid	A.J.D
9.30 A.M. 26.9.15 TUNBRIDGE WELLS	Divine Service on COMMON with 200 lt. Infantry Bgde & attached Units.	A.J.D
9 AM 27.9.15 TUNBRIDGE WELLS	Field work at RUSTHALL COMMON.	
2 PM	Route March RUSTHALL – LANGTON – GROOMBRIDGE – BROADWATER FOREST.	A.J.D
9 AM 28.9.15 TUNBRIDGE WELLS	Infm drill on COMMON. Lectures on Sanitation & on Medical & Surgical Equipt.	GCW
2 PM "		A.J.D
9 AM 29.9.15 TUNBRIDGE WELLS	Field work at BROADWATER FOREST. Lectures on equipment. Instruction in packing wagons.	A.J.D
2 PM "		A.J.D
9 AM 30.9.15 TUNBRIDGE WELLS	Route March ERIDGE – ROTHERFIELD – MAYFIELD – MARK CROSS – FRANT	A.J.D

Forms/C. 2118/10.

CONFIDENTIAL

War Diary of

Major A.T. FALWASSER

Commanding 2/1st Home Counties Fd Amb.
R.A.M.C. T.

From October 1.15 to October 31.15

(Volume 1.)

Army Form C. 2118.

WAR DIARY
or
INTELLIGENCE SUMMARY.
(Erase heading not required.)

Instructions regarding War Diaries and Intelligence Summaries are contained in F.S. Regs., Part II. and the Staff Manual respectively. Title pages will be prepared in manuscript.

Hour, Date, Place	Summary of Events and Information	Remarks and references to Appendices
9 AM 1.10.15 TUNBRIDGE WELLS	Lecture on Stretcher drill on COMMON	
2 PM "	Lectures on First Aid & Sanitation & on Medical Equipment at Head Quarters	A.D.S
9 AM 2.10.15 TUNBRIDGE WELLS	Rotary Parade Kit inspection	A.D.S
9 AM 3.10.15 TUNBRIDGE WELLS	Divine Service on COMMON with 2nd & Infantry Bde R.F.A, A.S.C. & 5th (H.C.) Sus. Sigs. Co. R.E.	A.D.S
9 AM 4.10.15 TUNBRIDGE WELLS	Field work at RUSTHALL COMMON	
2 PM "	Unit paraded 1½ hours for inspection by operation of Inoculation Wounds. 12 men were subsequently interviewed by Inoculation expert of whom 9 were inoculated for Inoculation work. Pro Kitbags not received from A.O.D	A.D.S

(73989) W4141—463. 400,000. 9/14. H.&J.Ltd. Forms/C. 2118/10.

Army Form C. 2118.

WAR DIARY
or
INTELLIGENCE SUMMARY.

(Erase heading not required.)

Instructions regarding War Diaries and Intelligence Summaries are contained in F.S. Regs., Part II. and the Staff Manual respectively. Title pages will be prepared in manuscript.

Hour, Date, Place	Summary of Events and Information	Remarks and references to Appendices
9 AM 5.10.15 TUNBRIDGE WELLS	Field work on COMMON.	
2 PM	Lecture on "Packing of Equipment"	
7 PM	Night march SOUTHBOROUGH — BIDBOROUGH — SPELDHURST — LANGTON — TUNBRIDGE WELLS. A33	
9 AM 6.10.15 TUNBRIDGE WELLS	Field work at RUSTHALL COMMON. Lectures on First Aid. Lectures to Nursing Orderlies. A33	
9 AM 7.10.15 TUNBRIDGE WELLS	Route March with Transport, troops halted at LANGTON — BUCKHURST PARK — ASHURST — GROOMBRIDGE — BROADWATER FOREST — HIGH ROCKS. Field work carried out, advance guard at BUCKHURST PARK. A33	

Army Form C. 2118.

WAR DIARY
or
INTELLIGENCE SUMMARY.
(Erase heading not required.)

Instructions regarding War Diaries and Intelligence Summaries are contained in F.S. Regs., Part II. and the Staff Manual respectively. Title pages will be prepared in manuscript.

Hour, Date, Place	Summary of Events and Information	Remarks and references to Appendices
9 AM 8.10.15 TUNBRIDGE WELLS	Field work at RUSTHALL COMMON.	
1 PM "	Lectures on Sanitation & Medical organisation with Bearer.	
6 PM "	Lecture & demonstration on loading & lashing of limbers re Nursing Orderlies & stretcher men. ADS	
9 AM 9.10.15 TUNBRIDGE WELLS	Battalion parade. Lectures on First Aid & Methods of carrying wounded. ADS	
9.30 AM 10.10.15 TUNBRIDGE WELLS	Divine Service on COMMON with 20th Infantry Brigade & attached units. ADS	
9 AM 11.10.15 TUNBRIDGE WELLS	Field work at RUSTHALL COMMON	
1 PM "	Route March PEMBURY – KIPPING CROSS – WADHURST – FRANT. ADS	

WAR DIARY
or
INTELLIGENCE SUMMARY.
(Erase heading not required.)

Army Form C. 2118.

Instructions regarding War Diaries and Intelligence Summaries are contained in F.S. Regs., Part II. and the Staff Manual respectively. Title pages will be prepared in manuscript.

Hour, Date, Place	Summary of Events and Information	Remarks and references to Appendices
9 AM 12.10.15 TUNBRIDGE WELLS	Field work on Common	
3 PM	Lecture on tactics	
7 PM	Night work BROADWATER FOREST — BRIDGE STATION — FRANT A.2?	
9 AM 13.10.15 ARROWE WELLS	Field work at BROADWATER FOREST	
3 PM	Lectures on tactics & Hinid?? bayonets	
7 PM	[illegible] A/(?) South trench received from Recruit Dep? SEVENOAKS A?	
9 AM 14.10.15 TUNBRIDGE WELLS	Field work with MG. Battn held well available	
6 PM	[illegible] to SOUTHBOROUGH — BIDBOROUGH — PENHURST —	
9 AM 15.10.15 TUNBRIDGE WELLS	PLATOON — RUSTHALL Rusthall — [illegible] & Co on [illegible] A?? [illegible] rendez[vous] at [illegible] COMMON. All C? A??	
6 PM	Motor cycle dis[patch] rider AM (Recruits)	
	Motor cycle rider for several depl. at SEVENOAKS A??	

WAR DIARY or INTELLIGENCE SUMMARY.

(Erase heading not required.)

Army Form C. 2118.

Hour, Date, Place	Summary of Events and Information	Remarks and references to Appendices
9 AM 16.10.15 TUNBRIDGE WELLS	Battalion Parade. Inspection of Protective Protection	
1.30 AM TUNBRIDGE WELLS	Battalion Dinner on COMMON. Walked on to old walks. Picking stones & heating up food	ADS ADS
4 PM — 11.10.15 AMHERST WELLS	Paraded at 3.30 AM. May it & Marches out. 201 of the walks. 56 horses mules and 20 vehicles and proceeded to starting point. VAD Hospital left of RUSTHALL COMMON. J's. i.c. of Infantry B'ds started from this point at 9 AM. Brigade Scout Ambu followed the rear platoon of the Bn. & pass the 46 E. Lancs Regt. halts for 10 minutes before each hour. Brigade halted for ½ hour at 11 noon at HOLTYE COMMON and then LANGTON — NEW TOWN — ASHURST — COWDEN — HAMMERWOOD CHURCH —	Refer ordinance Survey ½ to 1 mile Sheets 39 & 34

WAR DIARY or INTELLIGENCE SUMMARY

Army Form C. 2118.

Hour, Date, Place	Summary of Events and Information	Remarks and references to Appendices
	— EAST GRINSTEAD.	
	EAST GRINSTEAD was shelled at 3 PM & men were [?] of shells in empty trucks. Three trucks were pushed in to open. Considerable difficulty was experienced with practically all the water [?] 3 days previously [?] [?] to [?] in place of ride & horse. All were [?] or [?] pulled to [?] & clear [?] of the fire by [?] little [?] that would & still be [?]. JK H to Antwerp which [?] had been intended to start at EAST GRINSTEAD at 4 PM travels at HARTFIELD & [?] was [?] to bring it in.	
2.3 AM 19.10.15 EAST GRINSTEAD	Paraded at 2.30 AM & proceed to starting point ½ mile South of F in FELBRIDGE. Hour started 7 AM [?] March 4A [?] to previous day. Strength 8 officers 197 other ranks, 56 horses & 20 vehicles	Reserve Ordnance supply 1" Hot. 39

WAR DIARY
or
INTELLIGENCE SUMMARY.
(Erase heading not required.)

Army Form C. 2118.

Hour, Date, Place	Summary of Events and Information	Remarks and references to Appendices

Four cars to be transported by rail to REDHILL to prepare beds for troops on arrival.

Motor Ambulance remained at EAST GRINSTEAD to effect repairs & reported at REDHILL at 5.30 p.m.

Route followed EAST GRINSTEAD — FELBRIDGE — NEWCHAPEL — BLINDLEY HEATH — GODSTONE — BLETCHINGLEY — NUTFIELD — REDHILL

White Car on a heavily laden lorry had half hour halt at lee worn for midday ration at about 2½ miles north of BLINDLEY HEATH.

Arrived REDHILL at 2.50 PM & proceeded to billets viz. FRENCHES & THE GRANGE ½ mile north of REDHILL and of REDHILL — CROYDON road.

2.50 following men fell out during the march & were dropped in Ambulance & were fit for all were disposed of & other [?] billets in or around REDHILL.

WAR DIARY
or
INTELLIGENCE SUMMARY.
(Erase heading not required.)

Army Form C. 2118.

Hour, Date, Place	Summary of Events and Information	Remarks and references to Appendices
9 AM 26.10.15	2/5 E. Surrey Regt. 3 men	
	1/6 " " 19 "	
	2/5 " The Queens Regt. 4 "	
	3/11 " " ? "	
	4/1 H.C.D. Ambce R.A.M.C 1 " ADS	
REDHILL	16 Hind & men in Reception of the following horses:	
	Situated east of REDHILL — CROYDON road, ½ mile	
	north of Haytell Hill REDHILL.	
	FRENCHES — H.Q Stores & filled for 94 men	
	1. THE GRANGE Reception Hospital & sleeping accommodation	
	for staff of Hospital	
	2. THE GRANGE Billets for 200 men	
	3. THE GRANGE " " 60 "	
	4. THE GRANGE Isolation Hosp., Reception Room & Billet	
	for 30 men.	
	All men of Unit employed on fatigues, cleaning	
	training, horses &c. ADS	

Army Form C. 2118.

WAR DIARY
or
INTELLIGENCE SUMMARY.
(Erase heading not required.)

Instructions regarding War Diaries and Intelligence Summaries are contained in F. S. Regs., Part II. and the Staff Manual respectively. Title pages will be prepared in manuscript.

Hour, Date, Place	Summary of Events and Information	Remarks and references to Appendices
7 PM 20.10.15 REDHILL	All men have been employed today on fatigues & ordinary training inspected. (ADS)	
7 PM 21.10.15 REDHILL	All men have been employed during on fatigues, no ordinary training carried out. (ADS)	
7 PM 22.10.15 REDHILL	All men employed on fatigues. Erecting Marquee Hospital Red X Hospital & clearing ground for V.A.D. Surrey No. 108. (ADS)	
7 AM 23.10.15 REDHILL	Bty route Lecture on First Aid at Station H. Qrs. (ADS)	
7 PM 24.10.15 REDHILL	All led Divine Service at St Matthews Church REDHILL with all Batts & Army Rpt. and visit to R.F.A. & A.S.C. (ADS)	
7 AM 25.10.15 REDHILL	Route March KERSHAM - FARTHING DOWN - HOOLEY - REDHILL	
3 PM	Hockey Equipment & demonstration on case (ADS)	

Army Form C. 2118.

WAR DIARY
or
INTELLIGENCE SUMMARY.
(Erase heading not required.)

Instructions regarding War Diaries and Intelligence Summaries are contained in F. S. Regs., Part II. and the Staff Manual respectively. Title pages will be prepared in manuscript.

Hour, Date, Place	Summary of Events and Information	Remarks and references to Appendices
9 AM 26.10.15 REDHILL	Stretcher & bearer drill carried out at BATTLEBRIDGE	
4 PM REDHILL	Lectures on Sanitation & First aid rendering at H.Q. of section A.D.S.	
9 AM 27.10.15 REDHILL	Drill work at BATTLEBRIDGE	
4 PM	Lectures & practical first Aid & Sanitation at H.Q. of section A.D.S.	
	Sham engagement A.D. nursed from A.D.S. A.D.S.	
9 AM 28.10.15 REDHILL	Route March with bearers CATTON POINT — MERSTHAM — SOUTH MERSTHAM — BLETCHINGLEY — NUTFIELD — REDHILL. A.D.S.	
9 AM 29.10.15 REDHILL	Stretcher & bearer drill & field work at BATTLEBRIDGE A.D.S.	
4 PM	Technical instruction to section H.Q. A.D.S.	

WAR DIARY or **INTELLIGENCE SUMMARY.**

(Erase heading not required.)

Army Form C. 2118.

Hour, Date, Place	Summary of Events and Information	Remarks and references to Appendices
9 AM 30.10.15 REDHILL	Battery Parade. Priest & Dist. Detaintion.	
9.15 AM 31.10.15 REDHILL	Attended Divine Service at St Matthew's Church REDHILL ADS to all Battr. E. Surrey Regt & 201th Regt. R.A.M.C. ADS	

CONFIDENTIAL

War Diary of
Lt-Colonel A.T. FALWASSER
Commanding 2/1st-Home Counties Field Ambulance
RAMC.

from November 1st 1915 to November 30th 1915

Army Form C. 2118

WAR DIARY
or
INTELLIGENCE SUMMARY
(Erase heading not required.)

Instructions regarding War Diaries and Intelligence Summaries are contained in F. S. Regs., Part II. and the Staff Manual respectively. Title Pages will be prepared in manuscript.

Place	Date	Hour	Summary of Events and Information	Remarks and references to Appendices
REDHILL	3.12.15		No entries during month ended November 30th 1915. A.D.S.	

Confidential

War Diary

of

Lieut Colonel A.T. FALWASSER
Commanding 2/1st. Home Counties Field Ambulance
R.A.M.C. T.F

From Dec 1st. 1915. to Dec 31st. 1915.

(Volume 1.)

Army Form C. 2118

3rd M.70. RGMC

WAR DIARY
INTELLIGENCE SUMMARY
(Erase heading not required.)

Instructions regarding War Diaries and Intelligence Summaries are contained in F. S. Regs., Part II. and the Staff Manual respectively. Title Pages will be prepared in manuscript.

Place	Date	Hour	Summary of Events and Information	Remarks and references to Appendices
REDHILL	31.12.15		Nil for month ending 31.12.15	A.D.S.

1875 Wt. W593/826 1,000,000 4/15 J.B.C. & A. A.D.S.S./Forms/C. 2118.

CONFIDENTIAL

War Diary
of
Lieut Colonel A.T.FALWASSER
Commanding 2/1st Home Counties Field Ambce
R.A.M.C T.F

from Jan 1st 1916 to Jan 31st 1916

(Volume 2)

Army Form C. 2118.

WAR DIARY
or
INTELLIGENCE SUMMARY.
(Erase heading not required.)

Instructions regarding War Diaries and Intelligence Summaries are contained in F. S. Regs., Part II. and the Staff Manual respectively. Title pages will be prepared in manuscript.

Hour, Date, Place	Summary of Events and Information	Remarks and references to Appendices
10 AM. 11th Jan REDHILL	Inspection of Unit by D.D.M.S. Central Force on parade seven officers three hundred and eleven of other ranks, forty nine horses & mules, fifteen vehicles. Officers need further practice in equitation. All ranks need more detailed instruction in their various duties. Elementary first aid instruction needs frequent & constant repetition as it is quickly forgotten by a few men who are not highly intelligent. A.D.S.	
11 AM. 24th Jan REDHILL	Inspection of Unit by Brigadier Genl. commanding 2nd Home Counties Infantry Brigade. On parade seven officers, one hundred & forty three other ranks, forty two horses & mules, sixteen vehicles. A.D.S.	A. Dalrymple Kerr O/C. Home Counties Field Ambce. 2/1st Home Counties Field Ambce. R. A. M. C. T.

(73989) W4141—463. 400,000. 9/14. H.&J.Ltd. Forms/C. 2118/10.

Army Form C. 2118.

London Mounted ? 2/1st Home Counties Field Amb

WAR DIARY
or
INTELLIGENCE SUMMARY.
(Erase heading not required.)

Instructions regarding War Diaries and Intelligence Summaries are contained in F. S. Regs., Part II. and the Staff Manual respectively. Title pages will be prepared in manuscript.

Hour, Date, Place	Summary of Events and Information	Remarks and references to Appendices
8.30 AM Oct 22 REDHILL	The Field Ambulance proceeded by route march to EARLSWOOD Station to entrain on proceeding to IPSWICH to join 58th (London) Division. Strength 6 Officers, 175 of other ranks, 43 horses and mules, 13 four-wheeled and 4 two-wheeled vehicles. Entrainment of horses and vehicles was carried out without difficulty.	A77
10.40 AM Oct 22 EARLSWOOD	Troop train left EARLSWOOD Station.	A77
3.30 PM Oct 22 IPSWICH	Train arrived IPSWICH. Detraining proceeded without difficulty. Horses were hooked in and whole unit	

Army Form C. 2118.

WAR DIARY
or
INTELLIGENCE SUMMARY.
(Erase heading not required.)

Instructions regarding War Diaries and Intelligence Summaries are contained in F.S. Regs., Part II. and the Staff Manual respectively. Title pages will be prepared in manuscript.

Hour, Date, Place	Summary of Events and Information	Remarks and references to Appendices
IPSWICH Sept 27.16	Marched from Station at 4 PM to proceed to quarters at the Workhouse IPSWICH. All Officers and other ranks of Field Ambulance accommodated in hutments small billets. A.D.C. stores accommodated, and horses and mules stabled, at the WORK HOUSE. Head Quarters and Stores are situated at the WORK HOUSE and central meeting is also provided there for all Officers of Unit. A.D. A.D.Silvester Lt Col O.i/c H.E.D. Hunter A.D.M.S. RAMC.	

www.ingramcontent.com/pod-product-compliance
Lightning Source LLC
Chambersburg PA
CBHW081503160426
43193CB00014B/2582